# Healing Waters

POEMS THAT HEAL

Sandra L. Ross

Copyright © 2021 by **Sandra L. Ross**

All rights reserved. No part of this publication may be reproduced, distributed or transmitted in any form or by any means, including photocopying, recording, or other electronic or mechanical methods, without the prior written permission of the publisher, except in the case of brief quotations embodied in critical reviews and certain other noncommercial uses permitted by copyright law. For permission requests, write to the publisher, addressed "Attention: Permissions Coordinator," at the address below.

**Sandra L. Ross/Rejoice Essential Publishing**

PO BOX 512

Effingham, SC 29541

www.republishing.org

Unless otherwise indicated, scripture is taken from the King James Version.'

Scripture taken from the New King James Version®. Copyright © 1982 by Thomas Nelson. Used by permission. All rights reserved.

**Healing Waters/ Sandra L. Ross**

ISBN-13: 978-1-952312-64-9
Library of Congress Control Number: 2021906229

# Dedication

REVELATION 21:4 (NKJV) SAYS, "And God will wipe away every tear from their eyes: There shall be no more pain. For the former things have passed away."

This book is for you, the wounded, the bruised and the broken hearted. It is your season of healing.

# Table of Contents

ACKNOWLEDGMENT..........................................ix
INTRODUCTION...................................................1
CHAPTER ONE:     Identity............................3
                 "Who am I?".....................3
                 "The Pretender"..............4
                 "Authentic".......................5
                 Words of Revelation:
                 Be You..............................6
CHAPTER TWO:     Anger and
                 Unforgiveness................11
                 "I'm So Mad!".................11
                 "Let It Go"......................12
                 "Padlocked"....................13
                 Words of Revelation:
                 Forgive and be Healed..15
CHAPTER THREE:   Lies..................................18
                 "Who Told You That?"..19
                 "Life In Retreat"............19
                 "It's Broken!".................20
                 Words of Revelation.....20
CHAPTER FOUR:    Wrong Connections.....23
                 "Soul Ties"......................23
                 Words of Revelation:
                 Strings Cut.....................24

| | | |
|---|---|---|
| CHAPTER FIVE: | My Story | 27 |
| | "Pretty Things" | 27 |
| | "You Just Don't Know" | 28 |
| | Words of Revelation: My Story is My Testimony | 30 |
| CHAPTER SIX: | Love | 32 |
| | "Retarded Love" | 32 |
| | "What is Real Love?" | 33 |
| | Words of Revelation: A Christ Love | 34 |
| CHAPTER SEVEN: | An Outsider | 36 |
| | "Rejection" | 36 |
| | Words of Revelation: Never meant to fit in | 37 |
| CHAPTER EIGHT: | Road to Healing | 42 |
| | "Freedom" | 42 |
| | Words of Revelation: My Journey of Healing/Free | 44 |
| CHAPTER NINE: | Prayer of Healing | 48 |
| | Additional Scriptures | 50 |
| ABOUT THE AUTHOR | | 52 |

# Acknowledgment

To my Lord and Savior, Jesus Christ, the giver of life, thank you. Thank You Holy Spirit for putting a press in my spirit to write and release this book in this season. This book was birthed in a season of consecration and healing and that was put on a shelf waiting for God's timing and we know His time is the best. Ecclesiastes 3:1 says, "To everything there is a season, and a time to every purpose under the heaven."

# Introduction

*HEALING WATERS: POEMS THAT Heal* was birthed when the Lord instructed me to go on a one-year consecration: no TV, movies, and not to accept any marriage proposals. Also, a restricted diet of only fruits, vegetables and grains. I had heard the Lord and I responded in obedience. Many doubted, but nevertheless, I stood on the commanded Word of God.

At the end of the consecration, it seemed like all hell broke loose in my life. What I did not know then was that the consecration was the preparation of my healing process. The pain had muted me, and its secrets were killing me. I did not know who Sandra was outside the pain because I was acquainted with pain and carried it around like a baby. During this season of my life, I was connected to an inner healing ministry and the leaders were ever so gentle and patient with my healing.

The Holy Spirit pressed in my spirit to take this book off the shelf and release it now. It is the season to do so. The Lord kept showing me people lined up in rows with their mouths opened, waiting in anticipation. Many people are hurting and living their lives in mute mode because pain, trauma, tragedy, abuse, denial and unbelief silenced them. Not talking about it does not make it disappear. In fact, silence can kill you.

"*Healing Waters: Poems that Heal,*" walks the reader along my journey of healing. It is an experience of conversations in poetic form and revelations from the Father. It is my utmost prayer that this book will open the gates and trouble the waters of your healing and give you a voice so that you can cross over the threshold into wholeness, restoration in Jesus.

Psalms 147:3 says, "He heals the brokenhearted and binds up their wounds."

CHAPTER ONE

# Identity

"WHO AM I?"

Who am I? I know my name, birthdate, family, and place of birth.

Again, I say, Who am I?

I am looking in the mirror and I do not see me. I see the shell of a person I have become because of life itself.

I am a chameleon that changes colors to adjust to my surroundings to survive.

I am so heavy-laden because I wear so many masks to deal with life tasks.

Who am I?

My masks are happy, strong, bold, anger, rebellion, smart, boyish, girlish, flirtatious, and aloof.

All these colors I wear, depending on the needs of that day.

Who am I?

Daughter, remove your masks, your colors...

Lord, I removed all my masks today and stand in all my bareness and nakedness.

I ask again, who am I?

My beautiful daughter, you are:

My greatest inspiration,

My best creation

The apple of my eye

More than a conqueror

The redeemed of the Lord

The righteousness of God

A joint-heir

A King's kid

Everything to me

The reflection of my love

"THE PRETENDER"

I am out of bed and getting dressed for another day.

Before leaving out, I look in the mirror and all I see is rejection, fear, anger, hurt, hatred, unforgiveness, confusion, and a lost little girl.

*Identity*

Realizing, I cannot, I cannot, go out into this world.

I open the door to my walk-in closet and there are shelves with so many boxes. There are boxes with different colors, shapes, and their own designs.

I say to myself, "Hmm... which box do I choose today?"

So, I pick a box and open it up. It's a mask of courage. The next box is a mask of holy and anointed. The third box is a mask of flirty. The fourth box is a mask of put altogether and the last box is a mask of happy.

There are so many rows and shelves of masks.

I pick the mask of strength because I am going to work and need strength just to make it through.

I put on my mask and I leave out ready to face another day.

I wonder what tomorrow will bring.

I wonder if I will be prepared for whatever it brings...

"AUTHENTIC"

Wait, you say it's okay to be me.

Am I free to live life without masks?

My masks kept me from losing my mind.

My masks prevented me from killing myself.

Oh, how I long to be myself, to be the real self.

I no longer have to measure up or fit in; no more looking, sounding, or acting like them.

The world or man is no longer my standard; no more boxes, categories, and a need for approval.

This groovy and I am moving in anticipation with such gratification.

That on this occasion, I stand in ovation, motivated to be me only.

To be for real... that I can be my true authentic self.

I don't like green, but I love blue and it's okay.

I scream, finally for the first time, I see me... and I dare to dream, to be different.

I'm my authentic me and I don't have to fit in...

I get it. I got it...I'm Authentic.

WORDS OF REVELATION: BE YOU

The Lord reminded me of three secular songs.

*Identity*

"I'm Every woman"- Chaka Khan
"Got to Be Real"- Cheryl Lynn
"Superwoman"- Karen White

Although these songs are secular, I have learned not to put God in a box. The Lord can and does speak to his children two-fold, the natural and the spiritual. The song, "I'm Every Woman," is a lie from the pit of hell. Its bondage, masks, people-pleasing, and pretending. Every woman is a chameleon that adjusts and fits in her surroundings. Simply put, she's not genuine. The song, "Superwoman," is portrayed in so many words as a woman wearing her cape and flying to the rescue. What a farce and not so real. A superwoman takes care of everyone except herself. She's everything to everybody, and in the process, she lost her identity. Candidly speaking, I was every woman. I was that superwoman and I literally lost my mind. "Got to Be Real," is a song of liberation. It commands you to know who you are and love yourself to love someone else. The way you think about yourself and your characteristics is your identity. When your perception of you is marred, how the world views you can be crushing.

# Healing Waters

When I went through my healing journey, the Lord removed all my masks. I felt like a turtle without its shell. Have you ever seen a turtle without a shell? It looks like a vulnerable little lizard. It makes the turtle appear bigger than it is. It is a pretender. I was never my true self. The masks are what I needed to survive and function.

So, I did not know who I was without these masks, shells, or different colors. What you see and experience as a child will make you who you are. If a child experiences a traumatic event, the brain, in a sense, shuts down and compartments the event. This event prevents the victim from remembering because without it, the person would have a mental breakdown. A person in a motor vehicle accident (MVA) may recall getting out of a car, but if the crash is severe, they will not remember the moment of impact. An abused child may form masks or other personalities as a coping mechanism, and they may not be aware of them.

My psyche was shattered and fragmented. Here I was without my mask. I was clueless. My

*Identity*

mind was empty. I kept saying, "Who am I?" I would ask the pastor and God. I would cry because I was an adult with no idea of who I was. I searched the Scriptures for my identity in Christ. The Lord would speak to me ever so tenderly and tell me that I am loved because His son Jesus died for me. I'm kind, artistic, intelligent, creative, and have a funny sense of humor. In these moments with the Father, I learned who I am in Christ. My identity, personality, and individuality are what make me unique. No more masks. I can be me-------Authentic. I am not a carbon copy of someone or what I should be. To be the real me is so amazing.

To be real is like being in a room full of people and the most comfortable person is the one that is being themselves. Think about this, a lion knows he is the king of the jungle and so do all the animals.

Be Real, Be You, Be Your Authentic Self.... It is Time...

HEALING WATERS

SCRIPTURES:

John 8:32, John 16:13
1 Peter 2:9
Psalms 139:14

CHAPTER TWO

# Anger & Forgiveness

"I'M SO MAD!"

ANGER IS LIKE A slammed door. Misunderstood and so angry. Provoked by the enemy and looked down with frowns by them that should know me.

Uptight and it's not right. I'm about to blow a lid.

Oh! I need to rid the years of unvented pain.

The tears stain my eyes. Lord knows I tried to hide it.

I ask, "When will it be my turn? When will my wrongs be made right?"

In hindsight, I hear the Lord say, "The battle is His and not mine."

I hear, "I will repay, and that vengeance is His and not mines."

"LET IT GO."

No means no! Violated! Intimidated! Controlled! Manipulated! You're crazy! You're lying! I didn't do it! You are a liar!

You did do it!!!! It did happen!!!!

I'm screaming and no one hears or believes me...

I am quiet, sad, crying, and dying inside.

Closed off, shut off, and uptight, doors closed.

You say, "Oh, she's mean," but did you ask why?

Why bother to tell? No one will believe me anyway. You made sure of that...

It is not my fault I was born. I'm just going with the flow of life. My heart is full of strife.

I write and draw. It's my only voice because you muted me.

Jesus, I let you in my heart and now you say, "Forgive."

Why! Why! It's not fair. I want them to feel every hurt, pain, and wrong they did to me.

Time passed and I feel stuck like it just happened to me today.

It's a heavy load. I can't bear to carry it anymore and I'm tired of this rut.

I will forgive when they say, "I'm sorry."

Tomorrow and life are not promised to anyone. It's but a vapor.

So, value life as if it may be your last day.

Lord, help me forgive, let it go, release, and wipe the slate clean.

I hear, "Clink! Clink!" The cage of my heart has opened, and I feel so free.

I never knew, nor did I dream. I could live life so free...

I no longer see the hurts, but I see souls...

I forgive, I forgive, and now I can live....

### "Padlocked"

Hurt padlocked my heart.
Abuse padlocked my heart.
Rejection padlocked my heart.
Trauma padlocked my heart.
I couldn't see the forest for the trees.

I couldn't see the blue skies for the dark clouds.

Pain padlocked my heart.

You said you loved me and I only hear you hate me.

You told me, "I'm beautiful," and all I see is unworthiness.

You said, "Come, its safe. I won't hurt you."

Betrayal padlocked my heart.

Never fitting in, kept isolated so one would know my secrets.

I live in threat with regrets just so that the secrets are protected.

I run. I hide in closets. I'm found, and you tell me I'm drama...No I'm not!

Trauma padlocked my heart.

I told you what he, she did and yet no one listened...my pain distanced me.

Hurt padlocked my heart.

I hated men, women, and mankind.

Oh! God! My heart is so padlocked.

I don't want to be this way, so I prayed and cried out for deliverance, for healing.

Forgiveness and truth unlocked my heart...

Do you hear the padlocks opening?? I'm free!!! I'm free!!!

*Anger & Forgiveness*

## WORDS OF REVELATION: FORGIVE AND BE HEALED

One of the greatest hindrances to my healing was forgiveness and letting go of anger. Pain was my normal and I carried it around like a baby. I would console it with justification. I protected my baby with vengeance and to let it go was mind blowing. I wanted all my abusers to suffer and suffer right now!! I lived by the three-rule strike and you're out. I had a speech I would give to those that wanted access to me whether we were in an intimate relationship or friendship. "If you hurt me emotionally or physically, I will hurt you physically," and I meant it. I did so many times. Living three-strike rules, I would cut people off and they were literally dead to me. If I saw you, I didn't see you. I held onto grudges for years and yes decades. I did this as a way of protection, but it only kept me in a state of perpetual unforgiveness and anger.

When I gave my life to Christ, I came as a sinner. I repented and confessed Christ as my Savior and I was forgiven. My mind had to be renewed. I remember trying to praise God and I was so hindered. I had to leave my offering at the altar and get it right with so and so first. One time there was this sister I called my holy ghost sandpaper because she rubbed my flesh. So, I went in prayer, telling on her to God and He had me to pray for her. My flesh didn't want to. You know it's difficult to pray for a person with a heart full of anger and unforgiveness. So many times, the Lord had me do this and in conclusion, compassion was birthed in my heart. I no longer looked at the person, but I saw them as Christ did.

I thought to let go of unforgiveness and anger meant they won. They were getting off free, so not true. Those that did me wrong were living their lives and I was still stuck on what they did. I had to release the need to get even because vengeance belongs to God. I had to trust that He's a just God. He will repay in His own time and His own way. In my prayer closet, I would ask the Father to forgive me for this and that. The Lord told me you need to forgive first so I can forgive you and that I needed to forgive on every occasion. Jesus told Peter to forgive 70x7, which eradicated my three-strike rule. I learned and now live in the fact that forgiveness is a choice but it's a requirement for every child of God. Unforgiveness and anger are siblings that are in rivalry to have a place in your heart. I exhort you to be so quick to forgive, let it go, and choose to be healed.

SCRIPTURES:

Matthew 5:38-48, 6:14, 18:21-22, 23-35
Romans 12:19

CHAPTER THREE

# Lies

"WHO TOLD YOU THAT?"

WHO TOLD YOU THAT you were naked?

Why are you ashamed?

For I am GOD, I see everything. You can't hide from me. I see it all.

There's not a place you can go to hide from me, for I'm in every place beholding the good and the bad.

If you go to hell, run to the hills and hide in caves, I am there.

I am Jehovah Shammah. God is there.

Be naked and not ashamed. It's safe for you to come out of hiding. Your shell, false facades, remove your masks and be you.

The devil has lied to you and you don't know who you are...

*Lies*

You are a royal priesthood, a holy nation, a peculiar people, the righteousness of God, created in my image and is fearfully and wonderfully made, more than a conqueror, an ambassador of Christ, living stones, the salt of the earth.

It's safe to be authentic, genuine...be you.

### "LIFE IN RETREAT"

The sky is blue and the sun is shining bright.

I hear the birds singing and the squirrels gathering food.

I take in the beauty of this day.

I exhale in relaxation, it's an ordinary day and I feel safe.

Wait!! ... Wait!!

The wind is blowing. The sky is turning dark and cloudy.

It's thundering and lightning.

My heart is racing. I'm breathing ever so fast.

Noooo! Not today! I'm afraid!

I withdraw into my shell and pretend it's not real. It's not happening.

I wait for the storm to pass, hoping it doesn't last long.

### "It's Broken"

I heard the Lord say,
"It's Broken! It's Broken!
Every word curse is broken off your life."
Glass shattering to the floor. It's Broken!
Word curses falling to the ground, losing their power.
I see. I hear words of life causing me to grow. Life is springing forth in me.
I am who GOD says I am.
It's a scam of the enemy. He's beneath me, for he's already defeated.
Your lies are null and void.
It's broken! It's broken!

### WORDS OF REVELATION:

Words have power and carry weight. Also, words can bless or curse, speak life or death, and add or subtract. We see this demonstrated when GOD spoke to the emptiness and it became something. Satan is the father of lies, deceit, untruth, and falsehoods. He knows who we are in GOD and immediately begins destroying us by murdering or killing our identity, purpose,

## Lies

and destiny through words! "You're fat. You're ugly and no man will ever want you. You're only good for eating, sleeping, and sh-----g! Those words caused death to my self-image and self-worth. It skewed my perception and perspective in life. Traumatizing as a child and carried into adulthood, those words were like a broken record that played over and over in my head. The song never changed and sometimes the DJ, Satan, would scratch the record of word curses spoken over me to the beat of condemnation. I believed every lie and was engraved in my mind. Giving my life to Christ didn't stop the record playing. It was difficult to comprehend that anyone could love me, to love myself and especially Jesus that loved me.

I recall having an open vision:

The walls in my bedroom were wood paneling and were covered in nails. Everywhere I looked, the walls had nails in them. I didn't understand what I was seeing, and I asked Lord, "What does this mean?" The Lord said, "Every time you say I'm not worthy, you put me back on the cross." So, all those nails represented all the times I said, "I'm Ugly. I'm unworthy. I rejected love and His love. I hate myself." John 3:16 says, "For GOD so loved the world, that he gave his only begotten son, that whosoever believeth in him should not perish, but have everlasting life." The Lord reminded me of this and said, "Sandra, I died for you because I love you. You are worthy." I'm forgiven. I'm not guilty and beautiful. I began to cry because I didn't want to keep Jesus on the cross. I needed to let Him die and rise in my life. So profound, that condemnation was saying the shedding of Christ's blood wasn't enough, but it is and still is today. There is power in the blood of Jesus. The death, burial, and resurrection of Jesus sets us free. This truth cancels every lie. Every word curse dissipates and falls to the ground, never to have power over you again, in Jesus' name.

SCRIPTURES:

Romans 6:4
Philippians 3:10, 4:8
Romans 3:4, 12:1

CHAPTER FOUR:

# Wrong Connections

"SOUL TIES"

SOUL TIES, SOUL TIES, my soul no longer cries.

I tried to forget and live without regrets.

Strings severed, first a nip, then a tuck.

I'm no longer stuck to her or him.

You have no more control of me. I belong to Jesus.

My soul is free, yes, free to be me.

I can achieve it and believe it.

I am free and oh, what a blessing it is.

All the mess that was left, deposited has been rejected.

No longer dejected, but accepted, my spirit cries out, "Abba Father, I belong to you."

No longer looking back, I'm not Lot's wife.

I have abundant life in Christ.

## WORDS OF REVELATION: STRINGS CUT

A carpenter took a piece of wood and created a boy puppet to fill his need for a son, which was a good thing. It satisfied him, but what about the puppet boy? A toxic soul tie or a relationship may appear or start initially as a good thing. But as time spans, you notice that only one person is benefitting, which is the making of a toxic relationship. The puppet master pulls the strings and the person that's being controlled and manipulated is enslaved. They're stuck, suspended in time, and unable to move on. The puppet can't think independently, have its own opinion, and move without its strings being controlled by the puppet master. The puppet boy wanted to be real, but the puppet master was okay with him as he was because he had ulterior, selfish motives. If the puppet boy became real, he wouldn't be needed anymore. When we're connected to someone that's a toxic soul tie, whether it's spiritual, emotional, or physical and it ends, you still feel a pull to connect or there's still something there whether they're in another state as if they're under a spell. Every connection, place, and person aren't for you. Therefore, we must pray for divine connections or relationships and to be in the right place at the right time with the right people.

Samson lived a consecrated life that came with specific directions. He met a woman named Delilah that he loved, but she didn't love him. Delilah's motives were wrong. She needed to know the secret to his power and anointing so she could get paid. The enemy knows who you are in God and will send destiny killers to destroy you, make you compromise, and sin. After a while, he let his guard down because he had the wrong connection. It was a toxic soul tie. He told her and lost his power.

King David saw Bathsheba bathing and he lusted after her. Bathsheba was married, but David didn't care. They committed adultery and Bathsheba became pregnant. They kept it a secret. David schemed and premeditated the murder of her husband, Uriah. David and Bathsheba married, but the child dies as punishment. We may pick people, but did God pick them for you? Needless tears and hurts we bear because we don't pray before entering into covenants with people. I see toxic soul ties as parasites, leeches, and ticks. You must remove it, cut off its blood supply, sever the strings and be free.

SCRIPTURES:

1 Samuel 18:1
Ezekiel 18:4
Proverbs 6:32
Matthew 22:37

CHAPTER FIVE

# My Story

"PRETTY THINGS"

Pretty house, cars, clothes, and smile; You say what a pretty family, my life is a calamity.

Pretty door, porch, and a lawn; has it dawned on you that looks are deceiving?

Behind my pretty house and pretty door,

I am not smiling and walking on eggshells.

You cannot tell; my makeup hides it well.

Shopping sprees, luxurious trips, and expensive jewelry,

I am his pretty accessory, a hood ornament of a car.

Sisters in church with their jealous thinking that I got it all; pretty things.

I am hurt and my heart is in pieces. He is keeping up with the Joneses.

To him, looks are everything. He loves pretty things.

It's having a toll on me, no joy and no peace.

Every gift comes with a price.

A 4 -4-carat ring and he cheated again, and I am not excited.

Pretty things are not everything, for I rather have a bubble gum ring and a husband that loves me and not hit me.

### "YOU JUST DON'T KNOW"

Why do you act like that?
Why did you do that?
You said let the past stay in the past.
You told me the past is the past.
You just don't know...
It's the past infiltrating my present, my today.
Aloof, distant
You said, "Oh, she's antisocial."
You just don't know...
Walls, fences, and fortresses to keep the bad people away

## My Story

So many monsters to keep outside, not safe if they get inside.

You see me today, but you just don't know... my yesterdays.

The hills, the mountains and the valleys I had to climb just to be here.

It wasn't easy. Sometimes I was called crazy by those closest to me.

Mocked and ridiculed by those shocked when I told my story.

My story is my history, of all I went through.

You just don't know.

Hush! Shut Up! No one will believe you!

Silenced and buried in my hurt

You just don't know...

My Story

Rejection, Abuse, Rape, Molestation, Incest, Verbal, Emotional and Physical abuse, Violated, Manipulated, Intimidated, Silenced, Controlled, Shame, Fear, Guilt, Abortion, Miscarriages, Barrenness, Sexual Confusion, Spiritual Abuse, Genderless, Mental Breakdown, Depression, Unstable Relationships, Mocked, Ostracized, Slandered, Isolated, The Black Sheep, Misunderstood, Labeled Crazy, The Invisible One.

You didn't know.... But now you do.

HEALING WATERS

## WORDS OF REVELATION: MY STORY IS MY TESTIMONY

My story is a record of events I experienced and told as my truth. A truth that I kept hidden because of shame, anger, and of a culture of hush! I had to get to a place of being healed to talk about my past. Various questions such as, "Why me God? Where were You when I was being abused?" were answered in the Father's presence, love, and Word.

Romans 8:28 says, "And we know that all things work together for good to them that love God, to them that are the called according to his purpose."

I went through what I did for a purpose. My pain has purpose. I didn't get the revelation overnight, but I held onto this Scripture. I prayed and confessed it. I would ask the Lord to give me strength when the pain felt unbearable. When I wanted to throw in the towel, all I could think of was the people that needed to know that Jesus is a healer and a deliverer. You can

*My Story*

be set free from the prison of your mind and be made whole. My perspective changed and I now can see the beauty of it all. That's why I tell my testimony without shame. My story is my testimony because it's anointed with my tears and pain. Jesus has healed me. Wherever you may be in your journey, just know and remember your pain has a purpose and it's bigger than you. Jesus makes everything beautiful in His time. Your story will comfort and minister to others as you allow the Father to restore you. Reach out and touch the hem of His garment.

SCRIPTURES:

Jeremiah 29:11
2 Corinthians 1:4
Revelations 12:11
Psalms 30:5

CHAPTER SIX

# Love

"RETARDED LOVE"

**M**Y RETARDED LOVE, MARRED by the stains of pain.

Refraining from love, afraid it'll end in misery.

Pain, rejection, and abuse is my story...

I agree my love isn't like Jesus; so many reasons why my heart has been caged for countless seasons.

Sure, we can reason, and you'll say it's treason, a great travesty against God Himself.

No self-doubt, I don't want to be like this.

I want to love like Christ...

Never have I experienced true love without strings attached, a healthy love of myself.

*Love*

Repeating what was imprinted in me as a child

Yes, I know it was a long time ago, but in myself, I can't,

I don't know how to love without suspicion or conditions...

My love is retarded.

I often pray, "Lord, teach me how to love like You."

## "WHAT IS LOVE?"

I'm confused. I hear and read about love.

But I ask, "What is love?"

It's foreign to me. I'm confused because love has meant some type of pain.

I love you, but I hurt and violate you.

You're my little girl, my favorite girl, only to be followed up with a confusing touch.

You tell me I'm special, but why do I feel dirty?

Why doesn't that word make me happy?

Instead, it makes me fearful.

How can I love when it caused me so much pain?

## WORDS OF REVELATION: A CHRIST LOVE

I asked the Father what love is, and this is His answer to me:

Love accepts, covers, understands, corrects, protects, and even hurts.

A hurt that later brings forth power, grace, and empathy.

The Father chastens those He loves. He does so to get us back on course and to mature us.

Love isn't what the world portrays. No, it's not superficial and if it's only physical, it's lust.

Lust is conditional and when it fades, it moves onto the next hot thing. Lust is an appetite that's never satisfied.

When Christ died, that's love.

Love is a sacrifice. It made it right between God and man.

You must have Jesus to understand love.

Love can be a mysterious thing and for some, it's been a grievous thing.

Love is patient and it's kind when it's genuine. It stands the test of time.

Love is not binding, nor is it contriving.

Love is refreshing, invigorating and the exalting of others.

*Love*

Love is free. Jesus died for you and me. He's our redeemer.

CHAPTER SEVEN

# Outsider

"REJECTION"

*I*N THE WOMB, UNCOMFORTABLE and insecure.

One lost before, are you unsure about me?

I made it full-term and I'm not like your firstborn.

He told me, "I wish you were deaf and not her."

I hear and speak. If I could, I would trade places with her if it means you'll love me.

Others got the first and third pick, just to make her happy.

I like blue and she likes green. Then she wants blue and I'm given green.

"Why!" I scream, "This is mean. Can't you see it hurting me?"

The first choice of everything, my input doesn't matter.

Why don't I matter?

After me, I'm still a baby and she came.

Sucked on your breast, pushed away to make room for her.

I never had a chance to be a baby.

I was blamed for everything, Oh how my heart sting.

I never fitted in. Why?

I was blamed for objects in her ears and blamed when she swallowed pennies.

Is it any consolation to you I'm the second born?

There was a lot of pressure to carry the first born and the third thru the sixth born.

Who's carrying me? The pressure was too heavy for me.

I tried, but I was a baby. I was a little girl with the weight of the world on her shoulders.

WORDS OF REVELATION: NEVER MEANT TO FIT IN

"The circle doesn't fit into the square. The box doesn't fit in the circle."

The right piece of the puzzle fits, but the wrong piece doesn't. It's so aggravating when the wrong piece gets mixed in with a puzzle.

Have you ever put a puzzle together only to realize near the end that pieces are missing? Oh, what a letdown it is. Every puzzler knows to sort the colors, edges, and middle pieces together separately. This process is called separating to be accepted by those things in the puzzle that are similar. Most families consist of parents and children. Children are referred to as siblings and are connected by the same blood line. That's commonality. Storge or familial love that's unconditional refers to the parent's natural love towards their children or siblings for each other. In the Bible, we saw accounts of families with real issues and were dysfunctional in the same way we see it today in families. Jacob favored and loved Joseph more than his other children, which caused distention and jealousy. Cain murdered Abel, his brother, in anger. Esau and Jacob had sibling rivalry and deception. Amnon raped his sister Tamar.

## Outsider

It's possible to grow up in a family and feel like an outsider and even wonder if you were adopted. In dysfunctional families, you'll find children labeled the black sheep, which is the troublemaker. The scapegoat is blamed for everything that goes wrong in the family. The perfect child is the one that thinks they were loved the most or pretends everything was perfect. It is all a fairytale in their mind. You'll also have the child labeled crazy or liar, just to make the family look normal. The invisible child is the overlooked or dismissed one. If you were labeled any of these titles in your family, I will share what the Lord ministered to me. We did not choose our families, but He did. He knew which family scenario was best suited for us to fulfill His purpose.

Jeremiah 29:11 says, "For I know the thoughts that I think towards you, saith the Lord, thoughts of peace, and not of evil, to give you an expected end." WOW! What a revelatory Scripture, so profound in that it helped changed my perspective. I was never meant to fit in. I'm different and you are too. Different in the fact, we were chosen, marked, and anointed. Get ready for this, it's going to blow your mind. We are chosen to be rejected, betrayed, abused, and not fitting in with the crowd. Our rejection has purpose and it's bigger than us. In fact, it never was about us. Jesus came to earth in human form. His purpose was to be rejected so that we may be accepted by the Father through the shedding of His blood. Jesus suffered many things on purpose because it was about us. Jesus is my master and as His servant, I was able to stop saying, "Why me?" I began to thank Him because it's not in vain, but it was intentional. It had purpose. We can only minister and comfort others in the healing we received. My life, seasons, purpose, and destiny are in the mighty and capable hands of the Father. I trust Him with the plan and my life. I had to go through what I did because people are hurting, trapped in their pain and past. So many people need healing and deliverance, and I couldn't let them down. The Lord is always mindful of His children. His thoughts and His ways are not ours. He's the potter and we're the clay. I stayed in His gentle, capable hands because I learned He's Father and He knows best. Joseph was rejected, sold into slavery, falsely accused, and forgotten in prison. But praise God!! Joseph realized it was part of a plan that was greater than him. His rejection had purpose and it was to save lives. No more trying to fit in and accepting that I was chosen on purpose to suffer, to be rejected so that I can help others, save lives. We're in this world, but we are not of this world. You are different because you are chosen on purpose for a purpose. Oh, what a blessing that is. You are not forgotten. You are accepted and God knows your name.

SCRIPTURES:

Isaiah 55:8
John 16:33
Romans 8:15
Psalms 94:14

CHAPTER EIGHT

# Road to Healing

"FREEDOM"

Before me lies a road with gravel, stone, and dust.

The road at times is narrow and wide with valleys and hills.

As I walk this journey, along the way I pass houses I once lived in.

Each house represents and tells a story.

I stop and look but don't stay long.

For you see, I'm on a journey and as I walk along, I continue to pass houses, never stopping long or looking back.

You see, the road is the track, the path to my future.

I had to endure a lot of things and like Manasseh.

God has taken away the sting of it all.

I can't forget and never will I; only God can.

I cry at each house and continue, for my past has no hold on me.

You see, my truth is my liberty, and some may not agree.

I've learned whom the Son set free is free indeed.

I no longer ask, "Why me Lord?" or "Why did it happen?"

I heard the Lord say, "It's not in vain."

So, I continue along the path, the road that lies before me.

I now know the past is the past, and my future will supersede my past.

I continue my journey without looking back, without anger, bitterness, or unforgiveness.

My heart is right, and my life looks bright.

I do not need to make it right.

My walk has turned into a skip like a child. Then I start running and smiling.

I'm running towards the sun light and it's so shiny and bright.

I'm running to Jesus. He picks me up and puts me on His lap.

Jesus bounces me on His knees, up and down.

I'm so happy and giggly.

Jesus touches my cheeks and says, "I'm so proud of you. You made it."

I say, "Yes, I forgave. I let go, and I gave it all to you."

Jesus then kissed me on my cheek and said, "My wonderful daughter, you have done well."

## WORDS OF REVELATION: MY JOURNEY OF HEALING/FREE

One day I sought the Lord in my frustration because I was tired of hearing, "God is going to take you on a long healing process." I heard these words repeatedly and wanted to be healed right now! I was living in Washington State, next to a beautiful meadow where God ministered and healed me. The Lord told me, "Inner healing is like taking a walk in a meadow and picking a flower. You don't know when or what flower is going to be picked." Then he had me look at an onion and said, "Inner healing is like an onion. I'm healing you one layer at a time my daughter." Then one day I was watching Forest Gump and the Lord told me, "Inner healing is like a box of chocolates." You never know what's inside until you take a bite. We may not be aware of things or issues of the heart, but God does. He knows the right time to deal with it. Father knows best and how much we can handle, just like an onion's fragile outer layer. As the onion is peeled, it releases a smell that's uncomfortable and causes you to tear or cry. The onion's purpose is to season the food, so you continue to peel it regardless of the discomfort because it's needed. To relieve the burning and tearing, take a piece of bread and put it in your mouth. The bread will absorb the odor, stop the stinging of your eyes, and allows you to continue to peel and cut the onion. The first couple of layers of the onion is bitter-tasting. The layer has a membrane on it that makes it a little tough. If you keep cutting, the core is the best part because it the sweetest. Although the onion initially gives off an offensive odor, the more you peel off the layers that are not needed, the smell decreases.

There is a reason for the pain and the healing process is needful so that purpose could be fulfilled. So, I continued to be clay in the potters' hand, and I ate the living Word of God. The bread of life comforted me (John 6:35).

## Healing Waters

The Father loves His children and knows where we're at in Him. I learned to trust the Lord and committed my past, present, and future into His hands. The Father truly knows best, and my season of healing was on His timing and not mines (Ecc. 3:1-3). I stayed in the presence of God, on my knees in prayer, and did a lot of fasting. God had graced me to see in the spirit and I saw wounded soldiers and saints on the battle fields. Some were on the front line and others in formation, foot soldiers. I saw people on crutches, broken legs and arms in casts, bleeding hearts, black eyes and bandages wrapped around their heads. I saw so many hurting people that needed to hear my story and be healed. If I gave up, that meant all the suffering and pain was in vain. God had promised me that he would turn my pain into power and give me double honor for my shame. I learned to walk in truth by acknowledging, repenting and forgiving as issues were revealed so I could be healed. Wherever you may be in your healing, trust the Father in your process. I promise you freedom is a beautiful thing and God will get the glory out of your life. You can be free and whole in Jesus' name.

*Road to Healing*

SCRIPTURES:

Ecclesiastes 3:1-11
Matthew 11: 28-30
Psalms 37:3-5
Isaiah 61:3

CHAPTER NINE

# Prayer of Healing

*I* HAVE PRAYED FOR YOU, the reader, that every page of this book is anointed with healing virtue.

Father,

May this book locate and be found in the hands of those that need a miraculous touch of Your garment. Father, I pray for every person that has been wronged, abused, or wounded. I pray for every broken heart and crushed spirit that they be healed, touched and revived in the name of Jesus. Father, you called Lazarus and told him to come forth out of the cave of death. The angels of the Lord would come down and

*Prayer of Healing*

troubled the waters at certain seasons for healing. I decree and declare that you come forth out of your cave of death, pain, condemnation, fear, and woundedness. I decree and declare that this is your season of healing. You shall live and declare the works of the Lord. Jesus, You died on the cross and committed into thy hands Your spirit. Jesus, You died for (your name), and I commit my mind, emotions, past, present and future into your hands. I cannot carry it anymore. I come to You and give every hurt and pain to you in exchange for rest, peace, hope and healing. I give it all to You today so that I may be healed. I forgive (name the people that hurt you), and let them go that I may be free in the name of Jesus. Father, take my stony, hard heart and give me a heart like Yours, a heart full of compassion that is quick to forgive. I desire a happy heart. Fill my heart with melodies about You. I give You my mind. Heal my psyche, emotions, and personality. Lord, I decree and declare a sound mind in Jesus. Peace be still. I know that You are God in their spirits. Every word curse is broken, never to torment you again in Jesus' name. You are not your past, but who Jesus says you are; a precious jewel I declare. Father, keep your children close to you, in the bosom of safety, love them like never before. Heal and take away the sting of every ugly experience and give them the joy of the Lord. I decree and declare beauty for your ashes. Your tears will become your praise. I see your healing, restoration, and wholeness. I see you free in Jesus' name.

Be encouraged. This is your season for healing. Trust Father, Daddy, with the process.

## ADDITIONAL SCRIPTURES

### **<u>Healing</u>**
Isaiah 41:10
Isaiah 53: 4-5
Jeremiah 30:17
1 Peter 2:24
Jeremiah 29:11 Philippians 4:6-7
Revelations 21:4

### **<u>Joy</u>**

John 15:10-12
Psalms 16:11
Psalms 30:4-5

Romans 15:13
Psalms 126:5-6
Isaiah 61:10

## **Peace**

John 16:33
Psalms 4:8
Isaiah 53:5
John 14:27
Philippians 4:7
Isaiah 26:3

## **Encouragement**

John 15:13
Psalms 27:12
Philippians 4:13
Ephesians 6:10
Joshua 1:9
Corinthians 12:9
Psalms 46:1

# About The Author

SANDRA L. ROSS IS a minister, teacher, intercessor, and poet. She is the author of "It's Raining Wisdom: The Golden Nuggets of God." Sandra has served in multiple areas in ministry, but her greatest love is for the broken hearted and those bound by pain from their past. Sandra is a true witness of the wonderworking power of God in her life. Sandra experienced the ugliness of abuse and all it entails. She lived life as a victim. But one day, she heard the words, "It's not in vain." With this new perspective, her life was never the same. No longer walking in shame, her mourning was turned into dancing and she was given beauty for her ashes. No longer life as a victim, Sandra is a survivor because wounds did not kill her but birthed in her a passion to see people released from the prisons of their pain and to be made whole.

HEALING WATERS

# Index

A

Abel, 38
Abortion, 29
abundant, 24
abuse, 2, 29, 32, 52
Abuse, 13, 29
accepted, 24, 38, 40, 41
add, 20
adultery, 25
adulthood, 21
aloof, 3
altar, 16
anger, 3, 4, 15, 16, 17, 30, 38, 43
angry, 11
animals, 9
anointed, 5, 31, 40, 48
anticipation, 2, 6
artistic, 9

*Index*

ashamed, 18
ashes, 50, 53
Authentic, 5, 6, 9

B

baby, 2, 15, 37
bareness, 4
Barrenness, 29
Bathsheba, 25, 26
battle, 12, 46
beautiful, 4, 14, 22, 31, 44, 46
beauty, 19, 31, 50, 52
bedroom, 21
believes, 12
Betrayal, 14
betrayed, 40
binding, 34
birthdate, 3
blamed, 37, 39
bless, 20
blessing, 23, 41
blood, 22, 26, 38, 40
bold, 3
bondage, 7
book, 2, 48

boyish, 3

breathing, 19

broken, 20, 21, 46, 48, 49, 52

Broken, 20

brokenhearted, 2

bubble gum ring, 28

burial, 22

C

carpenter, 24

caves, 18

Chaka Khan, 7

chameleon, 3, 7

characteristics, 7

chastens, 34

Cheryl Lynn, 7

children, 7, 38, 39, 40, 46, 49

chocolates, 44

Christ, 9, 15, 16, 19, 21, 22, 24, 32, 34

comfort, 31, 40

comfortable, 9

compartments, 8

compassion, 16, 49

comprehend, 21

conclusion, 16

*Index*

condemnation, 21, 22, 49
confessed, 15, 30
confused, 33
confusing, 33
confusion, 4
conqueror, 4, 19
consecration, 1
consolation, 37
Controlled, 12, 29
corrects, 34
courage, 5
covenants, 26
covers, 34
crash, 8
creative, 9
cross, 2, 21, 22, 49
crutches, 46
curse, 20

D

Daughter, 4
death, 20, 21, 22, 48, 49
deceit, 20
deception, 38
declare, 49, 50

decree, 49, 50
defeated, 20
dejected, 24
Delilah, 25
deliverer, 30
denial, 2
deposited, 23
Depression, 29
designs, 5
destiny, 21, 25, 40
devil, 18
discomfort, 45
divine connections, 25
door, 5, 11, 27
dream, 6, 13
dysfunctional, 38, 39

E

empathy, 34
emptiness, 20
Encouragement, 51
enemy, 11, 20, 25
enslaved, 24
eradicated, 17
exhort, 17

*Index*

eyes, 11, 45, 46

F

fairytale, 39
false facades, 18
falsehoods, 20
families, 38, 39
family, 3, 27, 39
Father, 2, 9, 16, 24, 30, 31, 34, 40, 45, 46, 48, 49, 50
fear, 4, 49
Fear, 29
fearful, 33
firstborn, 36
flesh, 16
flirtatious, 3
flirty, 5
flower, 44
foot soldiers, 46
Forest Gump, 44
forgive, 13, 16, 17, 49
Forgive, 12, 15
forgiven, 15, 22
forgiveness, 15, 17
formation, 46

fragmented, 8
free, 6, 13, 14, 16, 22, 23, 26, 31, 35, 43, 46, 49, 50
freedom, 46
friendship, 15
frowns, 11
full-term, 36

G

garment, 31, 48
Genderless, 29
genuine, 7, 19, 34
ghost sandpaper, 16
girlish, 3
Glass, 20
God, 1, 4, 7, 9, 14, 16, 17, 18, 19, 25, 26, 30, 32, 34, 41, 43, 44, 45, 46, 49, 52
GOD, 18, 20, 22
grace, 34
gratification, 6
ground, 20, 22
grow, 20, 39
grudges, 15
Guilt, 29
guilty, 22

*Index*

H

hand, 45
happy, 3, 5, 33, 36, 44, 49
hatred, 4
healed, 17, 30, 31, 44, 46, 48, 49
healing, 1, 2, 8, 14, 15, 40, 44, 45, 46, 48, 49, 50
Healing, 2, 42, 44, 48, 50
Healing Waters, 2
healthy, 32
heart, 12, 13, 14, 16, 17, 19, 28, 32, 37, 43, 45, 48, 49
heavy-laden, 3
hills, 18, 29, 42
hindered, 16
hindrances, 15
hindsight, 12
holy, 5, 16, 19
Holy Spirit, 2
hurt, 4, 13, 14, 15, 28, 29, 33, 34, 49
Hurt, 13, 14
hurting, 2, 37, 40, 46
hurts, 13, 26, 34

I

identity, 7, 9, 20
imprinted, 33
Incest, 29
infiltrating, 28
inner healing, 2
insecure, 36
inspiration, 4
intelligent, 9
intercessor, 52
Intimidated, 12, 29
invisible child, 39
isolated, 14
Isolated, 29

J

jealous, 27
jealousy, 38
Jehovah Shammah, 18
Jesus, 2, 9, 12, 16, 21, 22, 23, 30, 31, 32, 34, 35, 40, 43, 44, 46, 48, 49, 50
jewel, 49
journey, 2, 8, 31, 42, 43
joy, 28, 50
Joy, 50

*Index*

jungle, 9
justification, 15

K

Karen White, 7

L

Lazarus, 48
leaders, 2
leeches, 26
liar, 12, 39
lies, 20, 42, 43
life, 1, 2, 3, 6, 12, 13, 15, 20, 21, 22, 24, 25, 27, 40, 43, 45, 46, 52, 53
lightning, 19
lion, 9
load, 13
Lord, 1, 2, 4, 6, 7, 8, 9, 11, 12, 13, 16, 20, 21, 22, 30, 33, 39, 40, 43, 44, 46, 48, 49, 50
love, 4, 6, 7, 21, 22, 25, 30, 32, 33, 34, 36, 38, 50, 52
lust, 34
lying, 12

## M

Manasseh, 42

Manipulated, 12, 29

marriage proposals, 1

masks, 3, 4, 5, 6, 7, 8, 9, 18

meadow, 44

mean, 12, 21, 37

measure, 6

melodies, 49

mental breakdown, 8

Mental Breakdown, 29

mind, 6, 7, 9, 15, 21, 31, 39, 40, 49

minister, 31, 40, 52

ministry, 2, 52

miraculous, 48

Miscarriages, 29

misery, 32

Misunderstood, 11, 29

Mocked, 29

motivated, 6

motor vehicle accident, 8

mountains, 29

mourning, 52

mouth, 45

movies, 1

*Index*

murdering, 20
mysterious, 34

N

naked, 18
nakedness, 4

O

obedience, 1
occasion, 6, 16
odor, 45
offering, 16
ornament, 27
Ostracized, 29

P

padlocked, 13, 14
pain, 1, 2, 11, 13, 14, 30, 31, 32, 33, 40, 45, 46, 49, 52, 53
parasites, 26
passion, 53
patient, 2, 34
peace, 28, 39, 49

Peace, 49, 51
perception, 7, 21
perish, 22
person, 3, 8, 9, 16, 24, 25, 48
personalities, 8
personality, 9, 49
perspective, 21, 31, 39, 52
pieces, 28, 38
pit of hell, 7
Poems that Heal, 1, 2
poet, 52
poetic, 2
potter, 40
power, 20, 22, 25, 34, 46, 52
praise, 16, 41, 50
pray, 16, 25, 26, 33, 48
prayer, 2, 16, 46
pregnant, 25
premeditated, 25
preparation, 1
pretender, 8
prison, 31, 41
prisons, 53
protection, 15
protects, 34
psyche, 8, 49

punishment, 26
puppet, 24
purpose, 20, 30, 31, 39, 40, 41, 45
puzzle, 38

Q

quiet, 12

R

racing, 19
Rape, 29
reason, 32, 45
rebellion, 3
record, 21, 30
redeemer, 35
reflection, 4
regrets, 14, 23
rejection, 4, 32, 40, 41
Rejection, 13, 29, 36
relationship, 15, 24
renewed, 16
repay, 12, 16
repented, 15
requirement, 17

rescue, 7
restoration, 2, 50
restore, 31
resurrection, 22
revelation, 30
revelations, 2
righteousness, 4, 19
rivalry, 17, 38
royal priesthood, 19

S

sacrifice, 34
saints, 46
Sandra, 1, 22, 52, 53
Satan, 20, 21
Savior, 15
scream, 6, 37
Scriptures, 9, 10, 17, 22, 26, 31, 41, 47, 50
season, 2, 45, 46, 49, 50
secrets, 1, 14
secular songs, 6
selfish motives, 24
sense of humor, 9
separately, 38
servant, 40

*Index*

Sexual Confusion, 29
shame, 30, 31, 46, 52
Shame, 29
shattered, 8
siblings, 17, 38
silence, 2
sin, 25
sinner, 15
sister, 16, 38
Slandered, 29
slavery, 40
smart, 3
smell, 45
soldiers, 46
song, 7, 21
sorry, 13
soul ties, 23, 26
souls, 13
speech, 15
spiritual, 7, 25
Spiritual Abuse, 29
sprees, 27
springing, 20
strength, 5, 30
strife, 12
strings, 24, 26, 32

strong, 3
subtract, 20
suffer, 15, 41
sun light, 43
superwoman, 7
survive, 3, 8
suspicion, 33

T

teacher, 52
tears, 11, 26, 31, 50
testimony, 31
three-strike, 15, 17
thundering, 19
Time, 9, 13
tragedy, 2
trauma, 2
Trauma, 13, 14
traumatic event, 8
treason, 32
troublemaker, 39
trust, 16, 40, 46
truth, 14, 22, 30, 43, 46
turtle, 8
TV, 1

*Index*

U

ugliness, 52
ugly, 21, 50
unbelief, 2
understands, 34
unforgiveness, 4, 15, 16, 43
Unforgiveness, 17
unique, 9
Unstable Relationships, 29
untruth, 20
unworthiness, 14
uptight, 12

V

vain, 40, 43, 46, 52
vapor, 13
vengeance, 12, 15, 16
Violated, 12, 29
virtue, 48
vision, 21
voice, 2, 12

W

waters, 2, 49
weight, 20, 37
wholeness, 2, 50
woman, 7, 25
womb, 36
word curse, 20, 22, 49
words, 7, 20, 21, 44, 52
world, 5, 6, 7, 22, 34, 37, 41
worthy, 21, 22
wounds, 2, 53
wrong, 13, 16, 25, 38, 39

Y

www.ingramcontent.com/pod-product-compliance
Lightning Source LLC
Chambersburg PA
CBHW052119110526
44592CB00013B/1669